THE STORY OF WATER

CAROLINE SAUNDERS

B&H kids

Nashville TN

Dedications

From Caroline
For Greer, who always got thirsty when we talked about this book,
who watches the raindrops race across the windows,
who longs for the day when Jesus will wipe away every tear.
I long for it too, buddy.

From Jade
For captain Conno, who steers the ship under the commands
of our admiral Jesus Christ. It's not a calm journey,
but shore-ly a safe arrival, for the Living Water is with us!
He guides us through, and we only have to follow Him.

Text copyright © 2022 by Caroline Saunders
Art copyright © 2022 by B&H Publishing Group
Published by B&H Publishing Group, Nashville, Tennessee
All rights reserved.   978-1-0877-5670-7
Scripture quotations are taken from the Christian Standard Bible®,
Copyright © 2017 by Holman Bible Publishers. Used by permission.
Christian Standard Bible® and CSB® are federally registered
trademarks of Holman Bible Publishers.
Dewey Decimal Classification: C220.95
Subject Heading: WATER / BIBLE. O.T. STORIES / BIBLE. N.T. STORIES
Printed in Dongguan, Guangdong, China, May 2022
1 2 3 4 5 6 · 26 25 24 23 22

There are twenty Scripture citations hidden in this book. Can you find them?
Read them in your Bible to learn more about Jesus, the Living Water.

In the beginning,
God invented water.

He said,

"Water!
Time to exist!"

and the water
obeyed.

The water happily
swirled across the
surface of the globe.
God said, "This is
good." And it was.

Later on, God invented humans. He said, "This is very good," and it was! The humans happily danced in the home God had given them.

Genesis 1

Humans were different from water.
Water can't laugh or leap or talk
to God. But humans can!

Genesis 1:27

Humans are special because out of all creation, they are most like God. That's why it is important for humans to obey God.

At first, everything was wonderful between God and humans—until the humans chose not to listen.

Genesis 3

Soon, humans were disobeying all the time, which brought more and more pain into the world.

Genesis 6:5

Thankfully, one man named Noah wanted to obey God. So God told Noah, "To punish all this disobedience, I will tell the water to cover the earth. But you will build an ark to float on the water. You will be safe inside with your family and the animals I send you."

Sadly, except for Noah's family, no one believed God would send the water. Their hearts were flooded with disobedience. They did not listen to God.

Genesis 6

8

Then one day, God said,

"Water! It is time!"

Genesis 7

The water listened, and it began to swallow the whole earth—
GULP!—drowning everyone and everything on the land except
for Noah, his family, and the animals on the ark. It was good
for disobedience to be punished, but it was also an awful day.

Weeks later, as the waters settled,
the humans noticed something new
in the sky: a rainbow! The rainbow
was a sign of God's promise to never
send death water again.

Genesis 9:13–16

Yes, God had a bigger rescue plan.
One day, He would rescue the world
with a different kind of water.

Through Noah's family, the world began to fill with humans again. God chose one family for an important job: to be His people and to show the world what He is like. This family lived in a country called Egypt. Sadly, Egypt's king forced this big family to obey him instead of God.

Exodus 2:23–25

So, God rescued His people from the king. On their way out, their enemies chased them until they reached a sea. The people were trapped!

Exodus 12:40–41

Then God told the water to do a new thing, and it obeyed. *SWOOP!* The sea stood up, forming two watery walls.

The amazed family walked to safety on dry ground.

Exodus 14

The family began a journey through a wilderness.
On the way, they became thirsty—and angry!
Why had God taken them out of Egypt just to let
them die of thirst in the desert?

God told their leader, Moses, to hit a rock, and
WHOOSH! Suddenly, water began to gush out.
The people gulped it down. They felt rescued
and refreshed.

But God knew the people's real problem wasn't
thirst for water. Their hearts were flooded with
disobedience, and they didn't listen to His voice.

This is why, one day, God the
Father told His Son, Jesus,

"It is time."

Exodus 17:1-7

Jesus listened and came to earth as a baby.
For thirty years, He lived a quiet life.

Then one day, Jesus went to the river to be
baptized as a sign to show He wanted to obey God.

As Jesus rose up out of the water,
God spoke from heaven and said,

"I love My Son so much!
I am so pleased by Him!"

Matthew 3:13–17

The people were amazed.

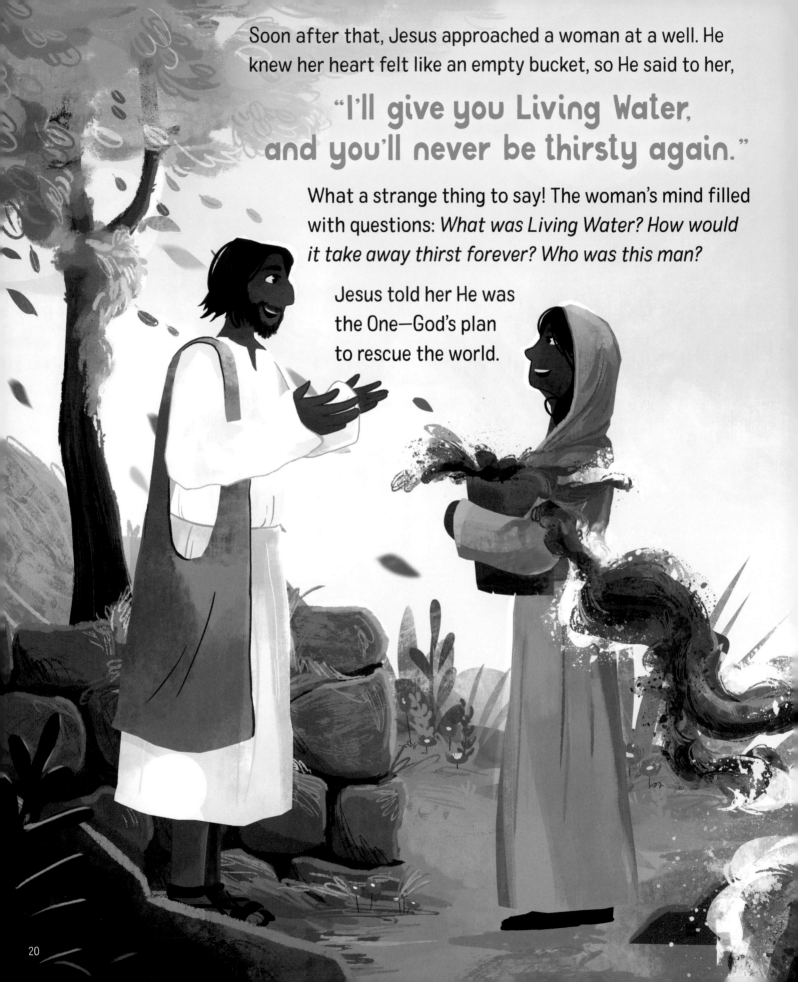

Soon after that, Jesus approached a woman at a well. He knew her heart felt like an empty bucket, so He said to her,

"I'll give you Living Water, and you'll never be thirsty again."

What a strange thing to say! The woman's mind filled with questions: *What was Living Water? How would it take away thirst forever? Who was this man?*

Jesus told her He was the One—God's plan to rescue the world.

The woman overflowed with joy! This Water would change everything, and she ran to spill the good news to everyone she knew.

John 4:1-42

People began to follow Jesus. They wanted this Living Water too!

One day, some of Jesus's followers were in a boat with Him when *BOOM!* A scary storm swirled over the sea. They thought the waves were going to swallow them up like death water! The terrified disciples went to Jesus—and found Him asleep. *Who could snooze in such danger?*

When they woke Him up, Jesus asked, "Why are you afraid?" Then, He looked at the waves and said,

"Stop it!"

The waves obeyed, of course.

Jesus's followers were amazed. They said, "Even the waves obey Him!"

Matthew 8:23–27

Once, on a crowded holiday when God's people remembered that long-ago rescue from Egypt, Jesus shouted:

"If anyone is thirsty, let him come to Me and drink!"

When the crowd heard His voice, some exclaimed in relief, "This is Him! The rescue we've been waiting for!" It was like hearing a gurgling fountain in a dry wilderness.

Others weren't sure. After all, He didn't have a sword or big muscles or a king's crown. "How can He be our rescue?" they asked.

John 7:37–44

Still others burned with hate toward Jesus. They grumbled in anger, "We don't want to listen to Him!"

Soon, Jesus's enemies were so angry,
they decided to silence Him forever.
That's when God the Father told Him,

"It is time.
I will pour out their
punishment on You."

Jesus thought about all the people. The ones
who loved Him, the ones who weren't sure
about Him, and the ones who hated Him.

And Jesus said,

"I will obey."

Matthew 26:36-46

Matthew 27:50

Jesus was the only human to ever obey all the way—
even when it was hard, even when His enemies hurt Him,
even when God's punishment poured out so strong that
His blood spilled and His heart stopped beating.

On the most awful day, the One with Living Water died.

The people who trusted Jesus felt all dried up inside.

But three days later, something amazing happened. God told the One with Living Water,

"Live again!"

And He did.

Matthew 28:1-6

28

Jesus's followers were more amazed than ever! This news that Jesus was alive was like being saved from an angry flood, like being rescued from an enemy, like slurping surprise water in the desert! When people heard it, they drank it in, like this:

Disobedience didn't win—*GULP!*

Death didn't win—*GULP!*

God has rescued us through Jesus—*GULP!*

The One the waves listen to listens to us—*GULP!*

AHHHH—what refreshing news!

Soon, Jesus went back to heaven
to be with His Father, but He said,

"Don't worry, I am sending the Holy Spirit.
He'll pour down on you and flow out of you
like water, so you have what you need to
show the world what God is like.

Acts 1:8–9

"Tell everyone about Living Water
rescue! Anyone who is thirsty can
come to Me and drink.

"And one day, I'll come back to flood the earth with God's love. There will be no more thirst, disobedience, or death. On that day, all the people who follow Me will dance happily in our forever home that gushes with Living Water."

Revelation 21–22

REMEMBER

"Let the one who is thirsty come. Let the one who desires take the water of life freely."—Revelation 22:17

READ

The Bible has lots of stories about water that teach us important lessons, like: God is in charge of every drop. Disobedience needs to be washed away. God is our great Rescue. Only God can provide for thirsty hearts. All these ideas flow together when we get to Jesus, the only One to obey all the way. Jesus's life, death, and resurrection make us understand these stories (and others) more deeply:

Noah and the Ark (Genesis 6–8). Just as the death water beat against the ark, Jesus was beaten and crucified to pay our punishment on the cross. God's rainbow was His bright promise: "I won't send death water again. I will send Living Water." Death water kills, but Living Water cleanses and heals. Jesus is God's new and better way to wash away disobedience!

The Parting of the Red Sea (Exodus 14). Just as the Israelites were freed from their enemy and brought to safety through the waters, sinners are freed from the enemy of sin and can live in God's care forever through Jesus. Jesus is God's way to deliver people from death into life!

Water in the Wilderness (Exodus 17:1–7). Just as Moses struck the rock in the wilderness so the thirsty people could drink, Jesus was struck on the cross so anyone who feels dried up inside can drink Living Water. In Revelation 22:17, Jesus says, "Let the one who is thirsty come. Let the one who desires take the water of life freely." Jesus is God's way to provide for people's thirsty hearts!

THINK

1. Humans should listen to God. But it's hard! Who is the only One who obeyed all the way? When do you think was the hardest time for Jesus to obey?

2. When Jesus died on the cross, it was awful—but it was also amazing, like slurping surprise water in the desert. Jesus took our punishment! We can't obey all the way like Jesus, but how does His obedience make you want to do your best to obey?

3. When Jesus commanded the stormy waves to be still, the men in the boat said, "What kind of man is this? Even the winds and the sea obey him!" (Matthew 8:27). That's wild! But here's something extra-wild: When you talk, Jesus listens. (He doesn't listen to obey you, of course. That's silly! He listens because He loves you.) Jesus wants you to talk to Him by praying. This is the biggest deal ever: the One the waves listen to listens to you. Whoa! What would you like to say to Him?

4. Jesus wants us to talk to Him, and He has plenty to say to us too. Where can we find His words? Why is it good to read them?